Poetic Essence

(Words Dance with Emotions & Imaginations)

S Afrose

Edited by Marie Ezekiel

ISBN:
Hardbound-978-621-470-390-6
MOBI/KINDLE-978-621-470-391-3
Softbound/Paperback-978-621-470-392-0

Published by:
Poetry Planet Book Publishing House
Rosario, Pozorrubio, Pangasinan, Philippines
Contact Number: 09554960094
Email: maritesritumalta@gmail.com

DEDICATION

For discovering the power of mankind---people must believe, this is the most important and magical spirit, to be an emperor of the Beautiful Life. This book is dedicated to them, to help, for holding that precious gem of humanity.

AT A GLANCE POETIC ESSENCE

Words fly, Words Dance, Words play, Words show---

Let's see. How can words fly? They come from the deepest cave of the mind and want to share

sweet fragrances. May be good or not, but that's not a matter. Words come to show

itself, the hidden vibe of life. This book "POETIC ESSENCE" contains so many dancers of words. They dance in different ways. Enjoy each part. Maybe, you have a chance to find out your sight. For example,

Writing, Poetry, Ray of love, Song of "A", Inner eyes, What do you want? My dear little sister, Stop there, Inside the dream, etc.

It's a great pleasure to share my emotions with the magic of ink. They come as my friends. They want to show up with their pride.

If there's anything, which may differ from your thought, then never mind. Don't take anything personally. I love to write poems. Poetry holds me as beloved.

Thank You so much dear God, for all the support. Thanks, dear all. Without all of your unconditional love, I can't able to make this colourful kite. I hope, you can make the time, to hold my book for showing utmost love. Pardon me, if there's any unexpected word.

May God bless me to move on all the time.

Amen!

TABLE OF CONTENTS

WRITING

Writing is such an art
For showering petals of words
With the power of ink
Rhythms of feelings.

Writing helps to revive
The beautiful aura of dear life
From the hidden site
To beat the upcoming strife.

Let the world know
Let the world see
The dreamy lane of writing
Without any more thoughts.

Gradually can be bloomed
A seed of a divine flower
A new season of life
As a writer at last.

May be good or not
That's not a big concern
Writing is such a part of the mind
Need to accept all--- so special!

1st Nov-22

POETRY

Poetry is my passion
To hold the dreamy motion
To cope with all mystic conditions.

Poetry is my part of the heart
I can feel its beats at all times
I'm so happy to get it here.

Poetry is my sweetheart
I can share my thoughts and love
By its integrity and love.

I can't imagine
How and when
It turns as a miracle part?

Now let me speak out
Let me shower
The hidden love of words.

1st Nov-22.

RAY OF LOVE

When mind cries
To get back its pride
Which once lost
Now need to find out.

Ray of love-

Hopeless mind
I'm here
Sitting and thinking
Merely can laugh.

Ray of love-

Hello dear
What's the matter
Can share
I'm your dearest friend.

Ray of love-

Searching
The source of voice
But can't see
Anyone?

Ray of love-
Close your eyes
Can feel
My existence
I'm in deepest mind.

Ray of love-

My name is poem
I can help to drench
Any kind of your pain
You will see a ray of love, at last.

1st Nov-22.

DANCERS

There are so many words
They come as trends in life
They are ready to speak
They want to show art.

What kind of art
Who can identify
Nobody as usual
Need the aroma of words.

Aroma--- wow
Incredible--- what
Can't wait to see
The hidden heart.

Who are there
Dancing all times
Dancers--- wow
Mysterious hut!

They come and dance
Artistic Essence of Poetry
Can enjoy this time
The era of Poetic hub.

1st Nov-22.

DON'T HURT YOURSELF

Take care dear
Don't hurt yourself
It's you and only you
Need to love.

You don't get
What do you want
You're depressed
Now taking the daring step.

Stop dear
Make it clear
So rare
Your life--- my dear!

If you think
By taking a break
Can make the vision--- so clear
Please, don't hurt yourself!

1st Nov-22.

STORMY DAY

The day was so good
When saw the lovely pool
Full of vibrant arts and colours
Easily helps to enjoy life.

Suddenly --- a strike
From the azure's hub
What was that
Thunderbolt! Ah!

The day turned into desert
The storm came so fast
No enjoyment existed
My mind suddenly collapsed.

Why?
Stormy day
Just a few moments
Making the dangerous lane.

1st Nov-22.

SWING

Swing Swing
A new string-
String string
A new tune-
Tune tune
A new song-
Song song
What's-wrong ?

Nothing Nothing
It's fine.
Come on here
Dear one.
You can see
The hidden treasure.
It's essential
To protect all times.

Life will be blessed
Life will be bloomed
Life will be wonderful
Life is the part of galaxy's pool.

2nd Nov-22.

SONG OF “A"

Amidst the vast universe
A little dream flies
At each part of earth
After all, it’s a part of paradise.

A bit more time is needed
At the end of day
Apart from the ray of dark
A little star of love.

At least take your time
Among all the rites
Adorable art of life
A song of the desired earth.

Are you ready to see
Are you searching for your love
At each moment of life
A Spark--- in deepest mind.

2nd Nov-22.

LYRICS OF LETTERS

As your wish
Be your beloved
Catch your mind
Dare to show up.

Each day passes
Face to face
Get your rider
Hahaha--- just enjoy this part.

Inside your heart
Jinx of rhythms
Keep up yourself
Love for all.

Mankind crown
Need to wear
Optimistic vision
Perhaps you lost once.

Query--- for what
Ready for the flight
See--- there's no ray
Till you have made your mind.

Ups-downs
Valid --- all times
When and how
X-ray--- for your thoughts.

Yes--- you have
Zigzag way--- now not a matter.
At each part of life
Be happy and hold the sail of life.

2nd Nov-22.

RHYTHMS OF " B "

Be my love
Beautiful art
Better to know
Because your mind is confused, dear.
Believe me
Be a part of lovely dreams
Brave to move on
Because you want to play any role.
Be ready
Be careful
Be strong
Because you need to accept any challenge.

1st Nov-22.

INNER EYES

Open your eyes
Those reside inside
Need to open
To see all the hidden sights.

The vast place
The blank canvas
Want to sketch
But can't decide.

So many options
Making you so confused
Don't worry
Take your time.

Optimistic vision
For your mission
Better to know
Each and every section.

Try and try
Without shedding tears
You will see
The golden sunshine.

(C) S Afrose, Bangladesh, 1st Nov-22.

WHAT CAN "C" TELL?

I'm the letter of C
My position is 3
Don't neglect me
I'm very useful to you.

Can say anything
How can show your passion
Control your mind
Look at there--- I'm lying.

Catch your dream
What's that reflection
It's your choice
Can conquer or not.

Look at there
My guitar of mind
I'm ready at all times
Cope on each part of life.

Can come
Can show
Congrats dear
Finally, you're here.

1st Nov-22.

CAGED MIND

How many times
You will cage
Your mind?

How many times
You will betray
Yourself?

How many times
You will lose
Your hopes?

Wait
Bow
Almighty God!

Relax
Feel
Beats of heart.

A voice
Don't be there
At last.

Let your mind
Come--- shining part
Of dear earth.

To know
Whatever
Tomorrow will be your pride.

Stand up
With beautiful mind
And enjoy.

Your smile
Shower
Thoughts of a lovely life.

1st Nov-22.

DELUSIONS

Deadly, they are coming-
Eagerly, I can't make any step.
Losing all positive things,
Unfortunately the collapsed art.
Sincerely I have made the way,
Illusions dwell all times everywhere.
Oh! Dear God, how can it be possible?
Nothing has seemed in my favor now.
Set up my mind to touch Your Blessings drops.

1st Nov-22.

FACE THAT LION

Here you give up
You don't want to walk
You don't want to show up
You want to sleep forever.

Face that Lion!

Roar and roar
Once upon a time
In your mind
The lost paradise.

Face that Lion!

The Lion's face
Let you know
Who you're
In a real sense?

Face that Lion!

It's your real form
Need to aware
No more tears
Face that Lion, dear!

1st Nov-22.

WHAT DO YOU WANT?

Leave me alone
I don't like
I want a break
From your site.

It's fine
Never mind
What do you want
Make it clear.

Tell me once
You don't love
You can't hold
Mysterious motion.

Dare to fight
All scary sights
Without any regret
I will sing.

You may take your time
Will be here or not
Just make sure
What do you want, dear?

1st Nov-22.

HOPELESS I'M

Hopeless I'm
Nothing can see
Nothing can think
Only void and vague.

Hopeless I'm
All things turn to meaningless
Pain covers my face
Life turns worthless.

Hopeless I'm
Blue colour is for what
It shows my painful heart
That heart can't beat now.

The world is a graveyard
I'm not here or there
Losing myself
At last, the lost mind!

Hopeless life
Spiritless mind.
Tune of heart
Lost forever!

3rd Nov-22

BESIDE THE FIREPLACE

Take a book
Sit on the chair
Beside the fireplace
Your mind lies.

The flash of mind
The flame of love
The book itself
Your golden part.

Take your time
To enjoy
Each moment
Without any hesitation.

Each word of book
Provokes you
As a friend
Just spend your moment.

The shiny art
Shadow on the wall
In the corner of dark
Your mind's trend lies.

3rd Nov-22

EVERGREEN TUNE

Lying down under the sky
Surroundings--- my lovers
I can't hold myself
A pristine love--- come on dear.

The wind comes with bare hands
Kisses my cheeks as a little one
I enjoy this time so much
By forgetting the unwanted life.

The sunny strike is also so adorable
I can find out the desired pool
Everything is so mesmerizing
Though life is a messy ward.

Heart and mind --- now happy
For a moment--- I was crazy
I lost my soul I lost my consciousness
Now can hear the evergreen tune.

That tune is in my heart
Helps me to heal all tormented parts
With this tune, I can feel and see
The staircase of divine love.

3rd Nov-22

MY DEAR LITTLE SISTER

Connection of two hearts
When it comes to the part
Brother-sister--- wow
That's love is so sweet.

My dear little sister
Don't cry
Look at me
Your elder brother.

You can share
You can see
Your shelter
Deepest my heart.

You're my only sister
For whom I can smile
I feel the meaning of life
Don't cry.

I will be there
When you need the hand of a supporter
Here or there--- anywhere
I will be your golden armour, dear!

3rd Nov-22.

SUCH A SMILE

She is feeling shyness
She is not ready overall
She doesn't know how can say
She is in love with dear earth.

Each day starts
With her beautiful smile
With the friend of sunshine
She loves to enjoy this part.

She makes herself
With a glorious phase
She will make a new era
By holding hands of sweet earth.

How beautiful
Her thoughts on life
So astonished
She will be in a harmonic hut.

Such a smile
Nobody can imagine
Fallen love with beautiful earth
Shower drops of happiness all over.

3rd Nov-22.

TUNNEL OF LIFE

Hold the sail of boat
Try to make this time
You will go so far
From here to azure's hub.

Tunnel of life
Always exists
For all
Don't hesitate anymore.

As a miracle
You will accept your words
From all sites of the universe
For telling the tale of life.

So many dangers
No need to go away
Must be there with your smile
The tunnel of life will hold your ride.

3rd Nov-22.

STOP THERE

Hey you
Stop there
Don't dare to come
I will fight
If you do as your mind.

It's my place
You're not welcome
You're not my friend
How do you say this
Just stop there!

What's your intention
May I guess
Your eyes say
You tell a lie
You have bad intentions.

I'm right
But I'm not afraid
I know how can protect myself
Dare to come
Then be ready to face my lion's face.

3rd Nov-22.

LOST MEMORIES

My sweetheart
Don't worry
I love you so much
The evergreen part of life.

Look at the diary
I have written
All the memories
Of our lives.

Once we were young
Now turn to older ones
We may be
But feelings can't.

Those are evergreen
Those spread fragrance of love
A beautiful life on earth
We enjoy any tiny part.

Lost memories
The essence of dreams.
Can't fade away
Those lovely moments.

3rd Nov-22

DON'T CLOSE YOUR EYES

Why and why
You're sinking
In the cave of the dark?
For what
For whom?
Don't close your eyes!

Here and here
A little child
Playing
With a kitten
How beautiful!
Look at the sight!

How many times
How much
You will deprive
From your imagination
Can't escape at all times.

Don't close your eyes
Open with a new vision
Can see Can feel
Your motion of life
For a moment--- smile!

3rd Nov-22.

INSIDE THE DREAM

The night falls
The moon calls
The dream comes
The mind wakes up
The heart beats
The hidden desire
Rolling.

Inside the dream
A new string
I'm with my dear
Can't go away
From this part
Now what
Enjoying.

Essence of dream
Aroma of love
Song of life
Mind dwells
With beautiful flies
Making a film
Inside the dream--- relax!

3rd Nov-22

GOLDEN SIGHT

Within nature's heart
Life swings as a little child
To see the golden sight.

That sight tries
To catch all
For accomplishing its goal.

Dear life
Can't wait
It enjoys the ray.

The sanguine sun
Never forgets
To scatter rays of life.

It helps
To lighten
Every dark site.

Sit on the swing
Now smile
Ready for the ride.

4th Nov-22

TWO PHASES

You and only you
Wear the mask
Sometimes jolly
Sometimes not.

Two phases-

Smile
Part of life
Not for long
It’s shattered as dawn.

Two phases-

Cry
Vast space
Making your art
Cover heinous parts.

Two phases-

It's obvious
Your part of life
Accept all
For the desired essence.

Find out your power
Hidden treasure
Can make
Your dreamy tower.

4th Nov-22.

OH, DEAR MIND!

Why don't you hear
Want to fly
By the ladder of hopes
From ground to sky?

Listen to mind
You need to think
To set your desires
Sequence to maintain Rhythms.

You can do anything
You can go anywhere
Your wings are so powerful
Never let down.

Oh, dear mind!
I will be happy
Hope you will also
By grasping my urge.

Thus a letter
Further may shatter
The dreamy hub
Hold your ruthless touch.

4th Nov-22.

POETIC LOVELY HUB

They always come
For dancing
To make rhyme
Of dearest life.

A new phase
Rainbow hub
Always exists
On azure's hub.

That hub revives
Colorful words
From deepest mind
With passion and love.

Yes
It's the mıracle
Rainbow calls
Never let down yourself.

Colorful site
It's your life
Though so rough
Still, be the poetic lovely hut.

Believe this
It's true
For the story
For your life.

Life --- oh sweetheart!
I want to see the rainbow
Then tell me one thing
Your thoughts--- colorful.

4th Nov-22.

MY BELOVED

From the very early life
You're my dear friend
Gradually time runs
My heart is lost forever-

My beloved
I can't express my feelings
My mind craves
To see the dreamy hub.

That tune was so sweet
When you told me loudly
" I want to spend my life
By holding your hands, sweetheart ".

I was shocked
Hearing your words
How beautiful
The whole earth!

Suddenly one day
A call from the hospital
By a road accident
You are no more on earth.

My breath is stopped
My heart is broken
How can I pass my life
It's totally impossible.

Oh, God!
Let me go
With my beloved
Without her--- I am not alive!

God cannot accept
I am wondering as a dead sou

l
From here to there
To search my beloved.

. 29th Oct'22.

DANCING "L"

Life
Love
Live.

Live
Lovely
Lasting.

Last
Let
Life.

Love
Literally
Like.

Lover
Look
Later.

Leave
Life's
Letter.

Learn
Lit
Little.

Let
Later
Labeling.

Love
Looking
Life.

Let
Life
Love.

4th Nov-22

NEVER

We
Want
What?

Heart
Hurting
How?

Mind
Means
Mum!

Oh
Opinion
Optimistic!

Never
Need
Nicely.

You
Your
Youthful.

Yes
You
Yearn.

Love
Litter
Life.

4th Nov-22.

AUTUMN VIBES

Orange colour
Decorates every site
As the flame of fire
It's autumn vibes, dear!

Come on all
Play your role
Don't show
You can't hold.

Surroundings full of new visions
Fallen petals make a new lane
Walking through that place
You can feel nature's heart.

Nature showers
Drops of love
From every part
For the new trend of earth.

4th Nov-22

DON'T WANT TO LIVE ANYMORE

You went away
From the very first.
I'm here as a tormented one
Can't hold this anymore.
Oh, God!
Don't want to live anymore.

Once made the hut,
Full of love.
So many colors,
No drop of tears.
Now all is over.
I'm in a graveyard!

Hey, you!
Don't do this.
I'm here I'm there
I'm in your heart.
I want to see your smile
You must lead a lively life.

Don't go away
Come on, dear.
Look at there
The rose of my love.
Take this
I will be happy, my dear!

4th Nov-22.

PAINTING

Canvas of mind
Make it fast
With all colours
For your imagination.
Now you have
Made the sketch
Reflection of Mind
So bright!

The painting is ready
You are happy
You see yourself.
So many colours
So many flowers.
Love --- lovely
Wow!!! Amazing!
The painting of dreamy life.

4th Nov-22

WAITING FOR THE ACCEPTANCE

Don't break your promise
Don't break my heart
It can't tolerate any more pain
You must realize.

What's my fault
Belonging to a poor family
But my love is eternal
It spreads the fragrance of sweet earth.

You know that
You must believe
You told me- "Don't worry
I never leave your hands."

Now what
You don't want to communicate
You forget all words
I'm waiting for the acceptance, dear!

4th Nov-22

OCEAN OF LOVE

The vast sky covered by dark
How and when can't understand
What's the next step
Need to find out the shining sight.

Hold the jeeper
Amidst the azure's hub
With passion and trusted support
Move it to see light.

Now the ray of golden sun
Can see from so far
It reflects the desired life
Beneath azure the bluish ocean of love.

Waves dance
Mystic Essence
Good or bad
All times, never mind.

When not like your pattern
Don't lose your temper
Remind the fact
Good and bad entwine.

4th Nov-22

I WILL STAND UP

It's fine
I will not cry anymore
I will accept all
As a part of life.
I will hold on
I will stand up
Though so tough
But I will be stronger
Better than past.
Don't know
How can face the upcoming phase
Still with a hopeful mind
I will stand up at last
To move on proudly.
Nothing can stop
My way of life
Maybe stuck
But still will try
To sing that
Song of lively life.

4th Nov-22

TO REACH

Oh God
Bless me
Love me
Save me
From every danger.
I know
You will
Because You love
Your creations.
Bless me to hold
My breath with great pride
To fight every danger
Without losing temper
To reach my desired goal.
Oh God
Now I'm shattered
To fight every war.
Need Your utmost support.
Hold me
In Your arms.
To help
Again to fight
With agility and love.

4th Nov-22

DON'T UNDERESTIMATE ME ANYMORE

This is not like before
I will not scare
I will not run away
I will try
Don't underestimate me anymore.

You think
I'm fool
I'm naive
I will not understand
It's not right.

Clearly visible
I'm not fool
I can see
I can feel
Your words.

It's time
To show up
To protect myself
That's why
I'm coming in golden armour.

4th Nov-22

HIDDEN FLAME

Hidden flame
In deepest shell
Of dearest mind.
After a long time
It comes
With a new vibe.
To show the world
Ready to make
The garden of life
With glittered pearls.

When someone wants
To see the world
With mind's eyes,
Can reflect
The hidden desire
For discovering
Precious treasure
Of dearest life.
It's obvious to all
Just need to remind
About the hidden flame.

4th Nov-22.

NOURISH MY HEART

Nourish my heart
With deepest love
Without any desire
Can believe forever.

I feel
Sinking
In the midst
Of lovely ocean.

I love this one
Love to drench myself
Without any stress
A moment is so special.

Motion of life
Essence of petals
From every site
Nourish my heart.

4th Nov-22

COLOURFUL HUB OF LOVE

The colorful hub of love
Scatters drops of love
Everywhere on this earth
Making all things so colorful
To utter only one word-
Just love--- for a colorful life!

A colorful life
Is desired for all minds.
Maybe here or there
But love can make
It with its power
Such a special one.

Rainbow can see
Day or night
Anytime Anywhere
If there's a ray
Of the true love
The soulful vibe!

4th Nov-22

ESSENCE FROM EVERY SITE

Essence of flower
Essence of nature
Essence of wind
Essence of wave.

Essence of dreams
Essence of love
Essence of imaginations
Essence of life.

Essence of words
To make colourful kite
You can play as usual
Without any more thoughts.

Now what
Essence of a lovely hut
Can touch each of the heart
From near to so far.

Are you ready
To feel the essence
From every art on earth
As God's love?

When you will think
As like that
Can enjoy your
Each and every moment.

4th Nov-22

STOP RIGHT NOW

Your greedy mind
Pls, stop all demonic desires.
Stop--- violence
Come on, in your real senses.

You can't depict
The tragedy of
The heinous deed
At last.

Stop to perform
Those deeds
As your entertainment
Stop--- right now.

When will take
The initiative,
Can be approached
Towards all with love.

5th Nov-22

DEAD TO ALIVE

From dead to alive
When touching --- the wave of ocean
When hearing --- the song of water
When seeing --- the bluish love
When reflecting --- the golden shade of dreams.

From dead to alive
When serene weather holds my heart
When dreams hold me all times
When thoughts are ready to spark
That spark is so special.

From dead to alive
When pen holds me to find out
Mystic tune of words
For the desired essence of life
A prestigious part!

(C) S Afrose, Bangladesh, 5th Nov-22.

SEA BEACH

The ocean's mart
All are beautiful arts
Mind enjoys
Heart beats with lively moments.

Sea beach
Here can see
The beauty of the sea
At a glance.

Taking some moments
With relaxation
Attention for what
Unexpected slot!

This provides
An opportunity
To enjoy
The essence of the sea.

Make your mind
Go there
With your pride
A beautiful ride.

5th Nov-22

LET ME SMILE

Don't provoke me
To say unless
You may hurt
And I can't help.

Let me smile
I want to show
So, what if I have no wealth
Can't I enjoy?

My life is only for me
Who are you to decide
I will say I will do
Whether cry or smile?

Let me say
It's my choice
It's my turn
And I smile.

You may go away
I will not mind
Better to say
I will enjoy my art.

5th Nov-22

IN FRONT OF THE MIRROR

In front of the mirror
Try to search
My real one
Who is beautiful
With its pride?
For a moment
Forgetting all pains
I may laugh
Is that me
Unbelievable!

Ouch
Now the real phase
Of this time
I have no option
I must survive.
How
That's a question
I love my life
Need to cheer up.

Pain
So pitiful
My status on earth
Still, I may love
In front of the mirror.

5th Nov-22

CAVE OF LOVE

Cave of love
For the beloved
Come on dear
See the golden shade
Of beautiful dreams.

CAVE of love
Only for you and your heart
Play the role
Not only yourself
But also for the world.

Cave of love
Helps to heal
All unwanted fears
Those make
To shed tears.

It shows
Ray of heart
The miracle
Amidst all parts
Of dearest life.

5th Nov-22

MY IMAGINATIONS

They all are my imagination
They help me to stand up
They help me to laugh
They help me to remind.

My imaginations
I hold the pen
On the paper
I write my words.

Each word shows
My dream to be alive
To fly with spirits of mind
As my beloved.

My imaginations
I hold the brush
The pellets of colours
In front of my eyes, a canvas.

I am making my earth
There--- so many colours
They spread the fragrance of a heart
My integral part of life.

After sometimes
Can see the ray of paradise
From the canvas
My dreamy hut.

5th Nov-22

TODAY IS A GIFT

Don't see the pool
Why and why
Today is a gift
Ready to wake up.

The pool is here
The pool is there
It's called the happiness
You need to be there.

Drowning
Breathing
Craving
Understanding-

Gradually
The pathway is visible
To show you
Just move on.

Today is another chance
Make it your sweetheart
Enjoy and live dear one
Happiness falls from every corner.

5th Nov-22

POETIC LOVE

Love is just a word
Its meaning is so vast
My love is exceptional
I love each letter of the mind.
Those letters come
With poetic chime
To make rhyme
Or as usual.

My poetic love
Making divine dove
They fly all times
My mind also flies.
It helps me to feel
It helps me to know
How can make yourself
For a better moment at last?

My poetic love
The precious treasure
Can't measure
Can't be vanished anywhere.
It will reside
Inside--- my mind and heart
To maintain those
Rhythms of life.

5th Nov-2

YOU CAN'T UNLOCK

Caged heart
Caged mind
Nobody can imagine
What's there in reality?
If you try
To unlock
Still can't
Due to delusion slots.

So many locks
So many keys
Only limited time
How can proceed?
Try and try
It's fine
Maybe once
The door will open.

Still, it's not clear
The answer isn't heard so sound
Valid --- why
Because heart and mind determine-
Never open
Doors of lively arts
Those are ready to go onward
For searching the way of paradise.

5th Nov-22

CAVE OF LIFE

Cave of life
Making its way
So far
From the vision of mind.

Cave of life
Need to fulfill
By colourful sights
To scatter ray of heart.

In heart
A cave also exists
It must want
The petals of love.

Love and love
Only can exit
In the cave of life
To make it --- colourful ride!

5th Nov-22

DANCING FLUTE

That flute is dancing
By using its magic
A spark--- in deepest mind.

That flute is singing
By using its tune
A splash of love.

Can't understand?
Wait-
Now close your eyes.

What can you hear
What can you feel
Can share with us.

We know
You don't
But why?

Just a simple flute
Your mind --- song of love
That comes from a lovely heart.

5th Nov-22

TINY ONE

Just a tiny one
Candle--- can shine
A part of darkness
With its calmness
As a hope, at last.

Don't underestimate
Any tiny thing
On this earth
Each one plays a special role
With its pride.

Need to know
Need to clear
All perceptions
Nothing is dead
Playing game, as alive.

Alive!
Yes dear
Need to show
The project of life
Within all parts.

5th Nov-22

A PART OF MASK

Just a part of mask
Wants to cover the truth of life.

Just a layer
Nobody even cares.

Just a quick view
What can it express?

No clue
Strong glue.

Busy to fight
With its right.

Still the same question
What's hidden?

Behind the mask
May I ask?

Pls tell me
I will try to realize.

5th Nov-22

FLOATING LEAVES

Floating leaves
Spread message
From Kingdom of Autumn
Be Ready
Never stop to welcome
The Desired hut!

That hut
Will be available
For all
To find out
The lost hope
And trust.

Floating and floating
Ground to sky
Everywhere
Though the way
Is so rough
Still can't stop.

5th Nov-22.

SWING OF GRAVEYARD

All alone
As a nightingale
Sit---
For a while
Wait---
For beloved.
But
Nobody can be here.
Only I with my heart,
Sitting on the swing
Of graveyard.
Ah!
What's that shabby wall?
A picture of past-
Two birds
Singing
With the tune of love.

5th Nov-22

AS A QUEEN OR KING

Lead dear life
As a queen-
It's your choice
Never regret
Just empower
Life --- as a part
Of dearest hut.

Lead your life
As a king
To make sure
Nobody will touch
Pain of life
From your site
Remind them all time.

As a queen or king
It's you and only you
You must believe this
You must trust dear God.

5th Nov-22

HEART-SHAPED WAY

A tunnel
Which is heart-shaped
There are so many shades
Of pink and violet.

Heart-shaped way
Shows the desired ray
So bright
You can feel your heart.

Love! Love! Love!
You better understand
Motion of life
Don't know--- why?

It's you and you
Want to go
Within this tunnel
By touching love.

Good luck
For this time
You will accept
Ray of life, all times.

7th Nov-22

BLESSED MORNING

Today is exceptional
When I saw the news
You can be here
Without any doubt.

Blessed morning
For me
Can't express properly
How do I start?

Dear God
Is the best
He will bless
Anytime.

Need to believe
Feel your heart
If you are ready
Then will be here.

7th Nov-22

REMINISCENCE

The most beautiful moment
When I was a little child
I could do anything
Nobody could punish me.

I enjoyed each time
To share my mind
To dear parents
They did love.

Grateful to dear God
For giving this wonderful family
I love them so much
I don't dare to depart.

Now look at the present
I have seen a lot of things
Around myself
What's that matter?

Everyone is here
Except for my Mom
She is in God's hut
How can I cope?

So tough to forget
It can't be
Reminiscence each word
Of dear Mom.

Yes
At last
I can see
The flashback of life!

Reminiscence!
For the youthful part
Of my dear life,
To lead lively onward.

7th Nov-22

PLS STOP RIGHT NOW

You want to tell.
Fine, carry on.
But one thing must remember.
When will take the step,
If can't,
Then don't rebuke me.
I will tell you,
Pls, stop right now.

Don't know?
Fine.
Never mind.
But don't waste time
To lose dreamy petals.
Show up
With passion
To hold the earth.

Otherwise,
Will be ready
To hear those words,
Pls, stop right now.

9th Nov-22

RED CARPET

Red flowers
The red colour of love.
Red blood
Unexpected flood.
Warning sign
Be calm.
Take your time
Never mind.

Those petals of flowers
Make the carpet of love.
For all of us with a muse of heart
Let's move on through the essence of love.

9th Nov-22

UNDER THE TREE

Feel free
Under the tree.
Talk with mind
Beautiful sign.
Carry on
Tree's love.
Gives you flowers
Gives you love.
Don't know?
Tree is absolutely
The friend of life.
Believe this all time.
Our planet
Full of vibrant arts.
Most of them
Are parts of trees.
It's not a word,
Save the future earth
By planting trees everywhere.

9th Nov-22

YOU'RE MY DREAM

You're my dream
The eternal glory.
You're my happiness
The colorful reel.
You're my heart
Beating for love.
You're my spirits
For the shining attire.
You're my mind
Hidden treasure.
I can't measure
The best gift of my life.

So many days have passed.
You don't come.
I can't manage my heart
It's not the real part.
You always stay
Deepest my heart.
You're my beloved
The spirit of inking shower.
Dear mother!
Memento of golden life.

9th Nov-22

SPECIAL TIME

This time is special
When I see my writes
Among all the arts
As drops of Dear God's love.

This time is special
It helps me to express
How happy I am
My mind is dancing like a butterfly.

The cute Butterfly
Tries to spread
My lovely words
Everywhere.

It is my friend
It inspires me all times
The spirit of my life
Holding it as beloved.

Yes
Of course
This is the best feeling
When you see your art.

9th Nov-22

SENSE

Go on proudly
Using the ray of heart
Your senses act as pillars
For building a strong world.

Be careful
When using each sense
Can't surrender
Till to discover the trend?

Sense
So strong
So week
Now what?

You can't take any step
Your thoughts tangled
How can protect yourself
Just wait.

Be ready
To think properly
Before taking any step
Your sense--- now smile as a friend.

9th Nov-22

WINNER

I'm a loser
I can't make up
I can't enjoy
I have lost my dreamy life.

Don't think this way
You will be a winner
Be positive
You will feel better.

When you smile
By seeing the sunshine
You pray to God
Look, you're enjoying, as a winner.

What do you want
No need to mention
Win- winner
If you feel your heart.

You love dear earth
You have a golden heart
It loves all
Without any expectation.

This is the best option
To mention your caption
You're the winner
This is the hidden treasure.

9th Nov-22

MYSTIC BIRDS

The tune of the violin
Helps to create
So many birds
A mystic site.

Those birds are flying
From the vault of violin
By making a way
Nobody can see, ever.

Hello dear all
Let's enjoy this tune
Playing with violin
So adorable.

Mystic birds
Wait for a while
I also want
To fly.

With my imaginations
I make my staircase
Now ready to walk
With the tune of the violin, at last.

9th Nov-22

ANOTHER RIDE OF LIFE

That clock acts
As a reminder
For all of us.

Everyone must remind
Each time when passes
Will not come back.

Need to use precisely
Each moment of life
Remind this.

Look at that clock
It's running
Never stop to show time.

When it will stop
Then can think
This is not working anymore.

It's dead
Ready to start
Another journey of its life.

Will revive
To use
The magic of heart.

Life is like
The clock
Can be stopped anytime.

Need to feel
Need to remind that
As a reminder.

By each of your deed
You can sow
Seed of immortality.

After the death
A new phase of life
By the reflection of your works.

If you dedicate yourself
Towards the lovely world
You will get the memento.

Just a legend
Be happy be ready
To enjoy another ride of life.

9th Nov-22

BIOGRAPHY

S Afrose (Sabiha Afrose); from Bangladesh. Father- Manirul Islam, Mother- Selina Begum. Educational achievements: B Pharm, M Pharm (Jahangirnagar University, BD). She loves to read and write. The journey started as the spirit of inker AFROSE SAAD (pen name). In this awesome section, she has achieved so many certificates from renowned platforms. Great achievement- Doctorate in Literature from Instituto Cultural Colombiano (Colombia). Her writes are published in magazines and so many anthologies (Intl.). 40+ anthologies have been published. Till now, she has published 4 solo Bangla poetry books and 2 solo English poetry books in Bangladesh.

On Intl. Platform:

Some of the published anthologies-

Spotlight, Dancing with Death, Women the Society Backbone, The quest for love, unity, and peace,

Inked with passion, Perception, Quintessence, Beautiful- in the eye of the beholder, Movement-our bodies in action, etc. 1st solo poetry E-book "Spirits--- Lively Life " from PRODIGY PUBLISHED USA(prodigylife. net).

"THANKS, DEAR GOD"--- First Published Solo Poetry Book from EVINCEPUB PUBLISHING INDIA (On Amazon, Flipkart, Evidence Pub.Com.)

Can reach her at afrosewritings@outlook.com sabiha_pharma@yahoo.com.

S AFROSE

www.ingramcontent.com/pod-product-compliance
Lightning Source LLC
LaVergne TN
LVHW010454160826
845677LV00012B/2478

* 9 7 8 6 2 1 4 7 0 3 9 2 0 *